BY THE SAME AUTHOR

From Island to Island
(Translated by Peter Cole)

QASIDA

HAROLD SCHIMMEL

QASIDA

TRANSLATED BY PETER COLE

ACKNOWLEDGMENTS
"Qasida" was first printed in Hebrew in *Hadarim* 10, Winter 1993.

Library of Congress Catalog Card Number 97-076785

ISBN 965-90124-0-3

IBIS EDITIONS
POB 8074
German Colony
Jerusalem
Israel

FORWARD

AN APOLOGY FOR POETRY, every so often one feels the same desire to set it down, not because poetry needs it (this much is *clear*) but because we do.... As for the engagement itself, one always asks *what for*, a mental soundtrack accompanying the entire mechanism of self and person. Virtually endless seeing, listening in a ceaseless flow, a touching that includes that of finger to finger on a single hand, the cycle of seasons one smells (the new moon of the month of Tammuz the height of the line from still-green to yellowing and finally straw), tastes in the mouth, not always with food. What am I leaving out. These are everyone's endowment. But we who note, who write, who gather, lovers of the paper itself, require from time to time an accounting.

–H.S.

QASIDA

1. The apparatus of poetry itself, which is to say *a poem* as a formal mode without center, *a qasida*. A concept of form for the complex poem, *the style of the qasida*, polyphonic, shifting, fickle.

2. True thought is construed through the form of the poem around the question of an "I". A storm of ideas, the heart's vision. Like a centipede, multiple voices. Deep depressions, hesitations, boasts, bold ascents on the basis of successful reconstruction of thought's figures. What else could justify the means if the end isn't relevant to poetry.

3. We identify not only the place in our having been there, but a chain-like series of associations follows with what we did, people we met, and even unvoiced thought-fragments of things that crossed our minds while we were there.

To this entire mechanism we'll grant the name *nasib* (the turning), and the place itself we'll refer to as the *atlal*. I turned my heart to give it direction (*nasabti et libi*), because this was the primary factor in the alteration of everything.

4. *The Solidity of the Past.* Because what happened once can't be retrieved. This is perhaps the principal meaning of "what was, will be". Which is to say, "it will be", in as much as it still is, so it will go on being. And not "history repeats itself", a fairly boring formulation.

5. *Re-joining.* And from there, the extension, the continuity of imagination's proliferation. A qasida as a handbook of poetry, and hence the Arabic meaning of the term, "poem".
Does it designate the form itself or a sketch of a notion of form.

6. A *desert* as a model of a world made concrete in erasure. "In-the-footsteps-of and falling behind." Erasure enforcing a trace of a kind. What once was, is no longer.

Mere chicanery. But the whole purpose of the movement was its after-image, an abiding impression as specter of what once was simple being.

7.   Remembrance as re-collection. Therefore the detailing of parts through a system of differences. Re-membrance as a joining of limbs anew.
Therefore, interludes of sensuality. Re-placement.

8.   The world as staging, and also the world as the staging of figures that once existed. Don't say merely (only) reality-presence. Say also an articulation of motion, a Kama Sutra of positioning.

9.   Pure wonder at the use of desert camps as significant location, departure as genesis. The *nasib* in its genius. As in a seance, a going-back to read the signs of life that is gone.

10.   The law of the thing is in the embodiment of thought as thought, hovering over particular examples in all their blatant actuality. There is no picture before

the eyes. There is nothing pre-established in writing to contend with. Spiritual ethereal "Law". The structure without a place of attachment. Unanchored. Shameless in its devices.

What did you mean by that.

11.   *The animal in the world of the qasida* is motion. "A trace" initially, belonging to the animal's trail. It's a form of boundaries-to-a-beyond, bridging place with place. As it moves forward, its presence already leaves a shadow-ghost behind. A trace, a track, an impression, a scent, a sign, and a model of the irresponsible.

12.   The wild animal exists in the qasida as an allegory of the domesticated animal. The camel's (the *naqa*'s) endurance is like ... the horse's bravery is like ...

13.   I'm speaking here about a "code" of innocence, like childhood's code. A code of sexuality. I'm inventing a pattern called "poetry", which I choose to call (for now, for a while) *qasida.*

14.   Presence/absence. Surely the qasida's bread and wine.

15.   The presentation of a condition (so it seems) that isn't unique but follows a model. Concepts like space and sheer endurance.

16.   *Atlal,* which leaves behind it a present like Jonah's gourd for the sake of a more solid and concrete past. Three stones, a few sticks, a scorched circle of blackness—this is the legend of "field" dictated by the still-readable remnants.

17. *Atlal.*   Draws the present beneath our feet. Embodies "not-here", elsewhere. So to the twin riders waiting it seems that the poet-hero-subject's soul has left his body, and they are obliged to call it back (to clear a way for it). This is a calling backwards.

18.   Not as in Joyce, where certain sights recall for someone "the purpose of the journey" but that in the qasida the sight removes all possible purpose for an

extension of the journey with meaning.

19.   So in the qasida recollection is what's already been learned, already experienced. But an active memory, as in Cavafy, the imperative, "Body, Remember".

20.   To know something "from the gut". What sort of things can one know in this manner.

21.   If we use the term "supportive pattern" to indicate a logical or conceptual structure which serves as a way of thinking in a certain area of experience, then the form of the qasida is an arch-supportive-pattern to all of poetry.

22.   To reconstrue, reread, air out the trace, bring something to mind, wonder, attend.
So the *atlal* is the priming bottle beside the hand-pump, to activate a pump with water in order to draw from it water.

23.   But what kind of memory, a kind of knowledge of how something passed in the past (more or less). Or the

other kind, when suddenly it seems that everything is happening again.

24. "The stomach remembers" somehow a more logical formulation, and this, precisely, is the subject of "the erotic interlude". How does Locke put it? To remember is to grasp something with the help of memory. Or consciously that something was known or apprehended from within.

Coleridge pushes the matter of "to remember" into a territory of kindergarten children and animals, which is to say "to recognize". Only a person, in his opinion, can be reminded.

But why, tell me, isn't memory activated in that one draws again, recollects in remembering the happiness one had, in remembering the dreams one came across. The initial motion of the qasida is a kind of "and then one reminded oneself somewhat, and afterwards said". To draw up, to revive or recreate a constellation of figures, a crystallization of ideas.

25. From the bounty of a series of women, three or four. The very ability to bring feeling to life varies

according to its intensity. On the qasida's menu it's easier to be reminded of a remarkably sour taste, or, on the other hand, of a sweet one, or bitter, than of the nondescript. Elevation in the qasida, which is clarity as differentiation, precision.

26. *Topography of the qasida.* Boundaries of its spread, its dispersion. The network of it, and its link to a broader topography in the world at large.

The names of places on a map and the places themselves with actual distances and qualities, and the names of places in the network of the poem with the differentiation and distance of its parts. Relation—as in internal connection—through focal separation.

27. Movement and occurrences in action underway along marked-out lines behind which one follows in the thicket of a network of words. Like the partial abstraction of a map. The last city to appear on top and what's north of it. The river that flows up against the limit of its banks.

28. The existence of the poet-speaker. The kingdom of flora and fauna, domesticated animals, women. The women linked as wayside stations on a journey. Eruptions into the landscape of invasive weathers.

29. Plot as shifting, plot as inter-tribal politics, plot as a broadening of conventional manner. Its destruction by necessity, weird desire, or simply braggadocio. Their taking upon themselves, for example, the full weight of revenge.

30. A battle as a form of conversation, like discussion.

31. *The pair of accompanying riders.* Often function like perspective in a painting. A window opened onto distant landscape, green leafage in the foreground as a means of gauging one's leap into space.
We require an official entrance into the landscape. We descend into it, slipping down off the animal while the companions, the riders, hold onto the saddled beasts and thereby bestow on the landscape (which one enters singly and then connects with) a mysterious widening.

32.   One always enters the past through a door (traces, signs) whose hinges are a present, a situation's links.

33.   *Qasida.* And in what sense is it a creation of a world. How is that world created. For example, take "the campsite". One stops at a certain place (but not any place) and in doing so establishes a presence, and thereby ropes off a certain space. Here.

34.   The complex movement. *a)* Actual arrival (the encampment) that turns into a reason for the widening into the personal pictorial space, torn off from reality.
b) A following of the absent tribe with its women. Try to determine their current location by means of extension, which is based on knowledge and circuits of possibility. *c)* The retreat or movement backwards in time (to lead time backwards) to cast a shadow on previous space. Enumeration by means of or through a rich panoply of theatrical choice.

35.   *Topos.* The small idyll or "epyllion" of the Alexandrians as a length (in fact "an opposing length"

in order to distinguish it from "epos"), and the length of a qasida. Compare Dante's canto.

36.   Al Jahat's comment that poetic content ("*al-ma'ani*") is scattered all along the road. The business of poetry is simply to choose from that content, arrange it, and give it order.

37.   The search for the actuality of experience in overtones and hints of meaning, ramification, and tone. But isn't that a definition of poetry.

38.   The *nasib*. A (contemporary) camp of one (singular consciousness) on a site (read: *atlal*) of the encampment that is no longer.
Which is to say, it contradicts absence with bolstered presence.   Presence, like a total absence of moon auguring the crescent of the new lunar month. Like a full moon, whose implication (after-the-fact) is diminution.

39.   Perhaps the chase after game in itself can serve as

a form of progression in the qasida. Haltings, scentings, alertness, patient waiting, disclosure.

40. A pure (if empty) background but *the fondest wish* of the poet-hunter in this instance is enforced presence of an absented actuality.

41. Undoubtedly the past is the "authentic". A formation of solidified amber. Its solid mass and not the "fleeting moment", that factual if haphazard flow of its adhesive substance.

42. The complex poem which is the qasida.

43. The powers of imagination are such (an advantage of disclosure) that its exercise can lead the poet to the "true site" of actual adventure.

44. It's clear to me how we whistle only old or borrowed songs. The story retold in the mother-tongue.

45. A surfeit of transformations against the ground of

the changeless, as in a sex manual.

46.   *Traces and erasure.*   "She trails her robe across our footprints." Embodiment and vanishings. Proverbs 30 (from memory), a serpent upon a rock, a ship's wake folding into itself.
Following after and falling behind.
A thin line of smoke-cloud rising and gone.

47.   Winds. Shifting dunes, sands shifting make light of the palpability of human footprints.   "She trails her robe across our footprints."   A couple, not yet having done what they're about to do (what both intend) and already busy erasing. Wiping out every trace.

48.   Strangenesses of sight in the desert waste. Lack of perspective owing to emptiness. What can one gauge dimension by.

49.   Hunters in a kingdom of "signs", those speakers of the qasida. Esau, "cunning hunter", "a man of the field", and Jacob plain, "dwelling in tents", a tiller of

soil.

50. Ostrich, "a camel bird", the largest of fowl. Indiscriminate gluttony, an appetite for hard materials which it swallows to aid digestion. Nonsense. Wives' tales.

51. *Point of view.* Riding on a camel (*naqa*) across the desert wastes, "in image a fortress". Tremendous size (in the desert's expanse) so it resembles a "mountain's peak".

52. *Traces, signs.* They're a kind of writing, in fact, that speaks of everything. They narrate.

53. *Testimony.* What. Who. For how long. This bush stripped of berries. A depth of dried-up channels indicates how much water has passed through, or something still damp somewhere.

54. The dung of animals, shed skin, a clump of scattered feathers signifying a slaughter. A trail of

blood, bodily emissions, a blob of saliva, secretion.

55. A fixed journey (*rahil*), it's clear-cut and at the same time a journey across a space which is a fragment of a longer journey, that crosses a lifetime which equates the *naqa* with man.
For the length of their days things overlap, a domesticated animal, a man, and a wild beast. Like when a lion regularly visits a specific cut of terrain, it wreaks destruction (it's the one that must be trailed). Eventually it acquires personality, a well-defined signification, character. Like those stripes, up above, on the outstretched wings of a hoopoe bird. With this coloration, this system of markings, this distribution of complementary colors.
Over there the daft activity of the woodpecker is its sign and signification. A kind of endowment of names prior to writing, which is to say, things in themselves, names in accordance with their qualities. There's no need to record it, to spell it out. It's desert legend, this quiet knowing. Registration.
At the mouth of a well, silver ornaments are scattered.

56.   A triangular recollection (in Imru al-Qa'is) of lovemaking.   A mother (and, accordingly, *possibly* a woman with child) in the course of her coupling twists her upper body toward her crying infant so as to proffer a breast.   An intricate behavioral situation, to say the least.

57.   Quotes of dialogue. Snippets of actual conversation trailing off in memory.   A hovering, resurgent presence passes over the landscape.

58.   *Atlal* (the charred site of the fire), where the poet-hero crystallizes absence.
"The expiration of the subject in the field of the other." This is how Ernest Jones spoke of "aphanisis", the apprehension that, God willing, we'll never know the absence of desire.

59.   A chain of lovers, episodes of erotic interludes. One want piled on another, or the lore of Don Juan, a wanting that was born from a previous time that manages to be answered by a wanting deriving from a

time to come.

60.   Thoroughly absorbed in the living moment of the poet-hero's evanescence. And thus engaged in reading traces of himself.
Like a cat twisting back at the defecation content of a hole it just dug.

61.   I'm not involved in any sort of "search for". I find. It's a matter of simply bending down and lifting up what's there.

62.   *Guide for the Perplexed.*   Never anything without "something else".

63.   A present longing for a future and a future drawn back to a past. This is all of man. Touching the last solid thing in order to regain a place to work from.

64.   A sign is not a sign until it is "readable". It first of all has to be discerned. This is the beginning of the *atlal.*

(A sign begins to be comprehensible to the poet-hero and in distinction indecipherable to the horsemen, companions on the journey, twin riders.)

65. For a moment one grasps it, in passing, and gives it the name "present".

66. Desire as a memory of desire.
Its refueling in the kindling of its memory. Memory fueled by desire. Desire is that which everyone already knows.

67. *Atlal.* The power of total loss rising up out of the aftermath of erasure.

68. The list of women as a simple series of memories associated with particular, concrete parts of the body. A victory-souvenir of limbs.

69. The qasida as a kind of bolero fisherman's net that the poet flings out from its folds across his left arm (toward a patch of desert landscape), thereby delimiting

for himself rocks and water and a prodigious slice of marine biology.

70. *Atlal.* A simple retreat from the flow of experience. Stubborn refusal of longing-in-motion. If you are not somewhat prepared to cease flowing, you will not gain access to the insinuating polyphony which is the exclusive right of your world of meaning.

71. The consciousness of the poet-hero passes (unceasingly) from muteness that is natural to it (the cipher of his heart's leaning) toward a readiness of speech, equally his.

72. The levant sparrow hawk seen through a friend's binoculars. Chest burnished orange, (suggesting the sun's influence) returning to the crest of a pine tree. Its back to us, its head a-swivel. What's palpable here is that "it always returns to the same place".

73. The concrete waits for nothing. You can be sure of this. Especially not for the poet-hero. Since it hasn't

the shadow of an expectation for the word.

74.   When he loses himself in listening's pose, drawn to the other's canopied departure, only then and under those conditions is he capable of discovering not-negligible treasure in the desert scape. Just a minute ago it all seemed loss and desolation.

75.   The transformation of what's desired becomes the basis for a treaty that's mouth-to-mouth, disillusioned but passionate.

76.   Not a taking stock with regard to what was, but a refashioning of a private past's structure as desire.

77.   At each instant of rewriting (ah unrelenting past) that which is created destroys the evidence of its predecessor. So that the process of erasure is continually drawn out and leaves behind it additional traces, fresh for a while. A free-flowing aggregation.

78.   Provide a stretch of provisional topography

(conditional) for the spreading out of longing's limbs and the province of desire.

79.   *Rahil* (pedlar: *rahel*, travelling from place to place, linked perhaps to "foot" or "leg": *regel*). Departure on the back of a familiar animal in its role in the chase, desire.
A moving semblance of desire-in-motion from the point of view of ground zero, that's where I am.

80.   *The poet-speaker-hero.* The human subject is empty, mobile, centerless.
At the site of the *atlal* he is "empty". In the passage to the *rahil* he is "mobile". And he is "centerless" in the conglomeration of scattered tribes and dispersal of wild beasts.

81.   Say: residual survival. Say: the infinite, unbridled nature of human desire.
Like a radio in an animated film. Strike it, smash it to pieces, stomp on it, it goes on playing.
Through the dance of two remaining wires in a final

broken lamp-tube sending the music out.

82.   Absence and presence as the wink of an eye, but intertwined. He's capable of stopping and seeing what's there before him only with the assistance of *what was there*.

83.   The lines live a life of their own. Never slack or bland. But taut, alert.

84.   And with this one awakens a sense of expanse, a quality of space, of congruence.

85.   The motion of a cult dance in a private enactment. Movement by movement like tracks left in sand. All is noted, and loved in its own right.

86.   You said qasida. To lay out a great number of diverse and strange things on a flat surface. Fluidity, yes. Intensity, of course. And fluctuating.

87.   Opposing forces, worked out in public, at full

speed.

88.   Is there a hierarchy of women in the qasida. The answer: "No."

89.   In order to properly understand the world of the desert (that which surrounds us), with the imagination's cunning create fictional concepts. Nothing is more important.

90.   Come what may, those waiting there on the backs of their mounts—let them be. They send us on our way, as though to kiss the fringes on the cloth of the Ka'aba.

91.   Who is it that continues to erase soul's landscape for us, who causes us to get up dawn after dawn, remembering not to forget the verbal formula.

92.   The *nasib*. What about the *nasib*. What emptiness are those camels approaching. The one just now descending is the troubled one, about to depart on the same journey backwards from current stasis to later. A

vital, unrelenting activity.

93. The sweep and rush of it. Call it *sandscape*, a culture of dunes.

94. Surveying the whole of the world for a handful of materials with which to compose the qasida.

95. As though a few meager and vague scratchings on the ground's surface augured a message.

96. Out alone in the desert under the sun, and solitude. On the way back find (odd as it seems) a piece of tomato that slipped out between two slices of bread, and miles of desert all around. And the feeling no one is there.

97. A window that in wisdom survives over time.

98. Writing, not that on the wall, but there beneath your footsteps. The faded pack of cigarettes you came across yesterday and come across again today. How

many seasons will it last before it survives "alone in memory".

The unique, the summation of all the encounters.

99. When we say "in a manner of speaking" it's clear to us *is it not* that everything is "in a manner of speaking". Better (with guts) to say, like the authorities of midrash, "There is nothing ... other than ..."

100. To ride out to a certain place in a western, or qasida, is to arrive from nowhere.

101. One thing is absolutely clear with regard to the desert mirage. It's one-sided. Explanation: You see the mirage but since the mirage isn't there at all (if this is the case) it doesn't see you (Lacan's tin of sardines).

102. You know virtually nothing about "desert". Admit it. Correct, I'm sure there's much more to know about Manhattan.

103. To alter nature through a series of small

adjustments in order to find ourselves. Wood that we gathered, piled up, and hid—found again untouched.

104. The most recent fire burnt down to glowing coals put out with a stream of urine. On the heap of stones rinsed and purified by rain, animals detect the scent of our presence.

105. Qasida. The entire range of speech's art, from the reflective to the emphatic.

106. *Qasida and memory systems.* These stones beside the same bushes beside the same rain-water channel, arousing what scene.

107. Walking through the poem, surveying which steps he has to take, but not actually dancing it, sketching it out, indicating.

108. Thoughts began with the word, that's where the whole sequence began as well. But what turns them into a sequence.

109. Do my reflections run alongside my speech as behind a mare, a colt. At all times giving heart to all the expressions of life within language.

110. A trip through unfamiliar terrain. Leaving an article of clothing on a bush or rock at various intervals in the landscape, to gather them on one's way back. Marking the landscape with identity.

111. Mne-mon. A suggested unit defined as the smallest physical change in the nervous system encoding a single trace.
According to the qasida's poetics, the time to begin to gather these memory units is when they are ripe, immediately.

112. "Wilderness," you said, where meaningful things stand out as distinct and isolated against a background of sameness. Small items in the landscape are name worthy; expansive distances go nameless.

113. Qasida. A kind of knowing and acknowledgment

of fixed value. An alteration of the shapes of the world's content from neutral objects to individual points of reference. The system itself is modest, the effects *far out.*

114. The site of a former camp (an existing site emptied of content) is the knot in the handkerchief one has to get past.

115. The twin riders are mindful, the moment the place is conceived of as an *atlal,* the subject of the qasida is deep in his thought.
This is like the moment when the orchestra conductor lifts his head, looks around, and readies his baton.

116. What is the practical meaning of this point in time, namely, the "stopping point" of the *atlal.*
The point itself isn't significant except as a springboard from which to leap, initially backwards, later forwards (or, if you'd rather, vice versa).

117. The view ("frame", "shot" in cinematic terms) in

the little window is the wisdom of the subject-speaker as a figure in a photograph.

118.   In our "reading" a landscape, remember and do not forget "distance". Keep the concept of an opening or "opening onto an expanse". Our subject-speaker is shut off within himself.

119.   Again the *atlal.* Is this analogy-inference, or site-sight, is it translation. Some kind of reflection. As if, with my own eyes, I'd seen an explanation.

120.   He sends out feeler horns, which is to say, illuminates what's ahead. Sends on lightning bolts of expansion over place and time. Does the same system apply to illumination behind. The illumination of the past.

121.   Just now the subject-speaker-poet is reciting idle thoughts to himself.
Get on your horse, hombre, and ride.

122. A poet activates a noun like "mouth" in his calling it (without pronouncing the name) a "cavern with teeth". Is this the archaic mode of language. A naive claiming of a given area (as if) and then back a few steps to the fixing of the word.

123. "Metaphor" is, perhaps, primitive. "The ship of the desert" for introducing the camel is somewhat childish in that it's based on the concept of a "beast of burden" being borne.
"Ship" is linked with journey, "desert" with concrete space, here desolate. Instead of desolate stretches of sea.

124. I write all this not about an actual qasida but create a concept for my own designs, to employ it consciously in an improper manner, the term "qasida".

125. What of the genre (the qasida's) overlaps with or even represents poetry in general. Is this like looking for hereditary resemblance between a child and the rest of his family.

126. But we'll concentrate on our talking about movement, characteristic habits of movement.
(How does one lift an arm, hold one's head, how to describe her particular way of moving forward. And how and to what extent does it grasp the reality of an exterior world.)

127. The complex women of the *nasib*. They have the same connection with reality that a bouquet of flowers has with real flowers in a real field. Nowhere else will you find them with the same density, proximity, combination, disposition in the world of action they represent.

128. *The women from the kingdom of flowers* establish the movement (each tries to catch the movement) of the flower's essence.
They are, perhaps, what a flower would never consent to be.

129. "An absence of vagueness, an absence of non-selectivity." The extent to which a dream is edited as

one returns to it. All return of this kind is misleading presentation. An incorrect description of a series of real frames.

But since this is the "partial presentation" that's given us, it inevitably becomes representative.

130. The firmness and smallness of the dung. Therefore resembling "peppercorns". What once resembled berries, soft, black, and oily.

131. Wounds on the surface that tell everything. Like a primitive African tribe of warriors, contemptuous of agriculture. As though "scratching the skin of our mother earth".

132. One of the things that "a question directed to myself" manages is a sharpening of the implement "question".

133. The common fate of man, in the qasida's jargon. From encounters and departures no one escapes.

134. The contraction to the itemized detail in a poetic description is like the depiction of an utterly unfamiliar object. Which is to say, it tries to remove all preconception, which is stored knowledge.

From this distance they might be horses or cows, even though I know only of mares and their colts grazing on that distant knoll.

135. Qasida. To the Graves of Lust one travels today and arrives in the past. The final tally is doing something full of nothing.

136. Because landscape is like reading words on a page. You can't absorb them all at once. You have to start from a specific place like Hockney-the-photographer from his unmistakable shoes with socks of different color. Is each separate polaroid photograph a "view".

137. *Nasib* always starts from a specific place, even though the qasida opens at the point where one "stops" to follow what once was there.

Since there's something that we refer to as the start,

there's something we can refer to as the start before the start.

Since something exists as "something", something also exists as "nothing".

138.   "Nothing" is the ground on which the qasida treads.

139.   The twin riders and the poet-speaker-subject on the ground of the *atlal*.   Both see the same thing but sense it differently.   "They" don't smell the smell that's there to smell.

140.   A charred hearth-stone, goat dung, a bush stripped of its berries.

Now I'll describe it differently.   Like the peculiar "equivalence" between things.   They tell the same story only because of their proximity.   The bush as it now is leads to a bush full of berries and the movements of departure.   The glide toward the departure (the *za'n*) whereward.

141. "Plants", "trees", "water channels". What they are, they are, name/definition. And even a sounding of the same name. And what they are to us. What they're linked to apart from themselves. The thing in its original primitive uniqueness and likewise the thing with certain liberties (with what will I be linked). Is this a game of world and subject.

I hear three things simultaneously. I may choose only one sound.

142. We're old hands at the expression of thought. Through these expressions we live, and within them.

143. Writing is a preying upon the world, so long as there's a subject.

144. Which is to say, everything, whatever you want, can serve as a point of orientation and organization, firm and abiding (or, in fiction, any point of view).

145. In language one can look out from various points of view and they are reflected in a range of

conceptual meaning.

Like a strip of landscape in Stifter. First you cross over, then you ascend the mountain for shifting views. A road climbs from the Sea of Galilee's lake line up to Ayelet HaShachar with its various vistas, now to your right, now to your left, of the same lake. All of them are authoritative comments as to what's below.

146.   Like wandering within the landscape of a Chinese painting. One time you take the trail to the right and another time you avoid it.

147.   Mistaken widespread use of the expressions "I always" and "I've always been", which hint at countless courtships and are almost always based on one time, or two or three (I'd wager).

Since it's impossible to go back on it or change it, we did it (said it) and continue to do it (to say it) endlessly into our present which advances into hands of the future.

"We had one like that also." *When. For how long.*

148.   What's the point of adding light to light.   How will you thereby multiply its sufficiency.

149.   Qasida (the concept qasida) has to be an inclusive summary (reduction) of all the qasidas (nothing less). The exceptions depart only from some non-existent model, not particularly useful.

150.   Such patterns as turning, waking, getting to one's feet, gathering one's clothes, are not the "desidera", but the habitual. So with the qasida and its structure, one can invert it, distort it, mislead it. Therefore one goes back to it.

151.   And it isn't a precise, axiomatic truth, without exception, that we require from a description, but something closer to "essence".

152.   Qasida as opposed to the unique trill (it's impossible to mistake it) of the blackbird. Finally understood as simply poem, song, hymn. Follow in its wake toward the polyphonic oeuvre of Lorca.

153.   The bedouin trackers as the qasida's interpreters of trace.   Reading evidence as a form of sight within and before the world.   And so with the dung of animals.   Its hardness, its concentrated blackness, its condensed quality, constitute a declaration like the bare oaks indicating a season.

154.   Sight, say, as promiscuity, as penetration.

155.   We try to get to the concept qasida in the way that a child arrives at the concept "tree".
Comment. It's possible to pay attention to the Marlboro pack on the path, but is it possible to know how many people lifted it in passing to check and see if in fact it was empty, to see if there might not anyway be something inside.

156.   And nevertheless, it is possible to know, "that's the branch where the hawk roosts", especially if it were there.

157.   To verify in a supernatural manner (the facts)

where we've been, where we're going, where we are, like the hunger of wolf cubs on the basis of their howl.

158. An imperative printed on a t-shirt, "Think Qasida". Which is nothing other than "read the world".

159. Think about the dismemberment and distribution of limbs (by turn) as a movement that constitutes the opposite of remembering. Like building backwards. Which is to say, dismantling the summer shack in the vineyard. A return to boards and nails.

160. If there's one thing qasida isn't, it's "stories about the past". They contain absolutely no sense of "in bygone days". Its path is immediacy, frequency, and the urgency of "this very moment", which is attained (in part) by "arrival" and "stopping".

161. This is remembrance as an act of will. The poet-hero-subject dismounts from his beast in order to devote himself to the ritual of remembrance, or the

"sign" announces itself as he speaks from himself to himself.

What the hero in fact does with that initial sign is another matter. The matter of poetry.

162. Signs as expression of announcement come only in the presence of a "reader".

163. It's no wonder that every departure holds a bit of *Cirque Medrano*. Tent meterage comes down with laundry line that supported family attire and animals are again collected as a sign of imminent departure. Just a bit of whitewash on a round stone, elephant and tiger dung. Splint and bandage took pity on the little horse's leg.

164. And where is the laughter and shouting, the embroidered canopy, and tattooed skin of limbs. Bare feet readied for the journey.

165. *Atlal.* Mute speech within as opposed to the *rahil*, an external process. A journey outward from an

inner drive. Painted memories that will not condone the continuation of the static condition. Like some young man who runs wildly through night-time streets, after the intensity of the film's footage.

166. Ask the question *what* pushes him forward. *Everything.* More fodder for the memory machine.

167. *Nasib.* After he's given permission to sink into his grief, they leave him alone. We don't hear him by chance. Beneath the chance we hear him.

168. An intensification of sexual encounters in the "erotic interlude" through techniques of splicing as in film. A sharpened focus accompanied by syllables of splintered conversation and heavy breathing. Think of Antonioni's *L'Eclisse.*

169. *Atlal.* Does this involve a gap in space. *No and no again.* It only seems so. A gap in the sequential emptiness, leading to presence.

170. How is it possible to learn one thing by looking at another. It's possible. By keeping your subject intact within you.

171. *The parts of the qasida.* The flexibility of material form. But even butter is made in a mould. Especially butter.

172. In this way typical images of the qasida like beads falling from a strung necklace with sexual overtones or (soft sensual innuendo) of loose clothing, licentiousness. Rituals of undressing in the erotic interlude.

173. A slackness of form in which it's possible to combine diverse parts indicates the fluidity of nomadic existence. Creatures who bind and unbind actually and metaphorically.

174. The horniness and promiscuity of the camel drivers is proverbial and well-tested. By night's light, gleaming teeth.

175.   Follow by the progress of your own thoughts, along the lines of another's.

176.   *Fakhr* (haughtiness, boasting to glorify the "I")—what is the arc of the boast's line. How to draw it. Is this boast "poetic license" dictated by the conditions of the form (the genre of the poem) or does it derive from individual impulse. Is it parallel to the face-painting and make-up of marriageable men in semi-primitive tribes. The boast as set design, or scenery.

177.   There exists a certain behavior, and a little conversation takes place there, sentence fragments back and forth, and a few activities that might be the sum of it.
These words under these circumstances have a meaning only as deep as the general mess of life, and this is precisely the goal of the qasida.   To resemble and imitate the density of that depth.

178.   What about transition. Transitions from part to

part do exist, but what kinds of transitions. How to characterize them. The conscious avoidance of fully articulated transition is also transition.

179. Literary criticism (like geology or archeology) gives the impression of being carried out on "solid ground" so long as it is dealing with the thing itself.

180. Among the unweighable evidence we can include the subtlety of tone, the sweep of vision, movement.

181. The apparent certainty of the first person, the lack of certainty of the third person, these, in the qasida, are axiomatic.

182. Once again I tried to read Brodsky's article, "Light in Venice." In the end it seemed ungenerous to do so.

183. *Atlal.* As in primitive cultures, first of all a mound of stones is turned over and then a mound of ashes. But with the coming of the poet-hero-subject spirits will hover over the ashes.

184.   All that I've written and noted and sketched so far is trying to say the same thing, like a thousand-and-one views of Mount Fuji.

185.   The problem of "everything flows" is exactly the point at which the qasida begins. A system of time is taken hold of, fluid to the point of absurdity.

186.   Like a play on the boards of a stage, the qasida has a time of its own (the poet-hero-subject marches three steps forward to activate the metronome), which is not a slice of historical time. Hence the irrelevant confusion that surrounds the provocative term "pre-Islamic".

187.   Attack the same thing from as many sides as you can manage. Like the loyal beast in Antara's poem, speared over and over again without letting up.

188.   It had a peculiar, anarchic tone as though it declaimed (o qasida) three roles simultaneously.

189.   Begin with the *atlal*. The salient thing is that it's directly before you.

190.   In thinking as in set design you need to know when to turn off the artificial lighting, to let the natural light take over. This is "discrimination", to know when the balance dips and the pans swing level.

191.   The passage from *nasib* to *rahil* (a journey to the "beyond") makes possible the embodiment of time.

192.   The structure of his pride is a superstructure, is like "once upon a time" in stories for children.

193.   *The trap of the aphorism.* That words take up their forms (find their places) prior to finding their full expression.

194.   Long live indeterminate meaning.   Worn out and shabby survives worn out and shabby.   A sliver of new moon, in its hands an old moon.

195.   Bits of old nesting inside a form which is a nest. That's how birds build.

196.   Take the image of the woman carefully "erasing our footprints" at the same time as we lay them down. "Our footprints" in what. In shifting tremulous sands.

197.   This "trailed robe" offers, perhaps, still more precise narrative facts for someone on the lookout for evidence. A ship, likewise a ship's wake.

198.   Question marks are "deep enough" only if they exist inside the words themselves.

199.   Qasida as a direction taken, never a one-way street.

200.   New traces over old traces. What serves as an example of the writing of one upon the other, or of the other upon the one.

201.   A bell's echoing lasts "a lifetime" (approximately). Like a novel properly read. What survives for the

sequential extent of a life exists.

202.   Again *atlal.* Here posing an endless number of irrelevant questions in the hope of cutting a breach through the compacted emptiness.

203.   *A multiplicity of overlapping women.* Improvisation without end, because no one fuck is like another. Undesisting repetition (with small variation).

204.   In order to pull it out whole "by the roots" one has first to loosen the surrounding earth. It's the other that you want, but attack this.

205.   Doesn't undermine, cancels value in that he screws a nursing mother in the presence of the child. Establishes new values, new emphases (what do I mean here).

206.   *Promiscuity* like the proclamation of the "I" in a dream, to invent another "self". The lovers' erotic foreplay is displayed by their complete withdrawal as if through a crack in time. Treacherous liberties.

207. Who said about the qasida, "Nothing is more important for the understanding of its existing concepts than to create fictional ones."

208. *The lovers' foreplay.* A situation conjured as by experiment. The qasida as a product of a flexible mind, or of what I've been referring to as "wisdom, a window." Through which light enters and exits.

209. *Qasida.* A form that is the "here" of a truth that is "there". This possibility that things in the world are linked by contrived attraction.

210. *Theory of poetry.* All the reader is capable of managing on his own, let him. But who is this "reader". The self-imposed delusion of a poet. An abstract notion toward which (among other things) one now extends a hand.

211. *The logic of its parts* (o qasida) or mere absence of linkage. Proximity and interdependence. Collision, attachment, reversal, fusion, concatenation.

212. *Method.* Take hold of the original idea in its form, the smallest, most miserable thing in all its poverty. *Now* let it (ugliness notwithstanding) proliferate.

213. *Qasida.* First of all a length. Interim as the meaning of the journey. Like a trip on a steamboat, not for the arrival, but the ports along the way. You have the same length (more or less) as a given, and find out what in the way of reality, and how much, one can take in with a toss of the lasso.
It's boarding a ship and knowing that for the next six days you will not set eyes on your destination. This is your domain, make the best of it. Therefore, "walks around the deck", "erotic interludes", "permissiveness".

214. *Making love.* (In euphemism) the infinite (in fact) number of times one can accomplish it. And, nonetheless, it's possible to understand someone who finds it "boring", that's a point of view. But "exhausting", *never*, for that's the gist of it.

215. The concept "verifiable" in relation to reality. One can go only so far in one's description of the *naqa*.

Thus far, no further. These are things one can easily check.

216.   *Mirage.* In the long and short of it, it's sight. We see what we see, whether it's there or not (and moreover others see it as well), and may confirm our claims.
What is the concept mirage for a camel.

217.   *Erasable* as a key word in the qasida. Call this "Jonah's gourd" or that which is destined for erasure. So we include in this the campsite, the character, even the most dazzling.
A twist of hair between her lips, Ingrid Bergman wakes, reaches for a late morning ring of the phone in Rio.

218.   What is the concept "key word". What exactly makes it necessary. "Key word" subsumes, gathers around it, groups of many concepts.

219.   *Erasure.* Wreaking havoc, but also total annihilation (as in time past) "to wipe out Amalek".

To scratch out, to scrape clean. In early examples perhaps a secondary form of "pulling out by the root". To blot out (what's written) "blot me, I pray thee, out of thy book which thou hast written" (what's engraved).

220. *Erasure.* The removal of recorded signs. It's also possible to talk about kinds of erasure, "total", "gradual", or "selective" (as in memory, as in dream).

221. A qasida is what space (in its most pleasant dreams) dreams of being.

222. Just as the qasida is a complex, not a simple, form, so the route it chooses for itself from start to finish isn't direct. "Circuitous" progress.

223. A qasida demonstrates a free, incidental kind of juxtaposition as in the waking dream. In its way, and its rhythm, it proceeds as it pleases, and this is exactly what the twin rider companions propose that the poet do.

224. *Always keep in mind* that one comes to the qasida's opening as in the Book of Genesis. The questions take the lead. So in the qasida one begins with a question, "whose abandoned camp is this".

225. *Time* solely as a unit of measurement, containing both former and latter.

226. That same tethered riding beast in the opening movements of the *nasib* appears again in the guise of the ghost-mare (*baliyya*).
I.e., the *naqa* of the fallen hero tied by its bridle to his gravestone and abandoned. And likewise the offering of the *naqa* on the altar of the *karim,* boundless magnanimity. Read: the moment's indulgence, beyond extravagance.

227. One very quickly enters the linguistic territory of the "detective story". Motives, evidence, clues, tracks, signs, details. A portion of specific circumstances of what happened.

228. Desert landscapes without ruins. About ruins one can speak only in the presence of architecture. Buildings, monuments, aqueducts, city walls.

229. *Form* as a nest or den of an animal, in which is couched a gazelle, a hare. "Form", exposed aspect of juxtaposition.

230. The poem's veracity depends on the choice of the given, in terms of *a)* a certain place in the space of the world, *b)* the qualities of a certain person such as the "I".

231. The "I" in the qasida is compound, a given of form. Comprehensive, malleable, taking up and dropping guises.

232. On the whole one learns from the meager native materials of memory's stock. As opposed to the scholar who checks diverse and extensive areas, in the course of his research.
As a "normal reader" judges a novel on the basis of

what remains with him after a reading, after sifting. While a critic sticks to the printed page, which gives him the license and privilege to employ each word.

233.   The plot of the film-script in its embodiment (the tested and ascertained facts). The fact's palpable excrescence.

234.   What once was, even though it is based entirely on distortions of memory, on cracks therein, and breaches, turns into plain fact.

235.   As with perspective exercises in drawing manuals, from the "thing-itself-in-reality" in straight lines moving outward that link it with its twin on paper.

This is the way of copying. The *naqa* in its gallop never breaks rhythm in its crossing from the sandy beach to the film's footage.

236.   *Syntax.* A positing of parts of speech like rivers, mountains, lakes.

237.   Dissected expression disguised as writing.

238.   An itemized list of that same hideaway dormer room with its bed chair table-lamp imitated via words within a form. These are objects disposed in space.

239.   The erotic interlude as guise. Trying on clothes, removing them, changing. The fabric lifted for a clipped instant over the body. Or as repertoire.

240.   *Camel.*   The primary requirement of nomadic life. *Mirage.* The ghostly spirit of a surface moving like a wave in motion. In Sanskrit, "the thirst of the doe".

241.   *Atlal.* If everything behaves as "significancies" for marks of a former site, you're already embarked on the qasida's journey.

242.   Promiscuity is the form in which certain exempla slide off from their normal places and take on the halo of summary representation.

243. Radical instances of personal behavior finally substantiate (in the long run-and-crawl of time) universal mores.

244. The qasida as a complex form that leans on a complex phenomenon, language. It demonstrates the ability to compound, language. How much ground can one cross with it. What kind of ground.

245. *Remember,* in the world of the qasida the heavenly pantheon is tied down by ropes.

246. "Understanding" as a deliberate stance under something, it doesn't matter what, for a specified time, as though under an umbrella for the rain's duration.

247. It's possible to talk about the positions of a sentence as positions described in a "sex manual". But these positions are fluid as well, over time.

248. Only reality can be "everything", perfect. The vocabulary in your dictionary is busy even now with the

task of perfection.

249.   The nature of a dictionary is such that it can never catch up with reality. As though the world keeps on inventing kinds of color, celestial occurrence, chemical reaction, disease.

The same is true for the realia of the qasida, and this despite its cultic limitation.

250.   It's interesting to note how the editors of the *Encyclopaedia Britannica* have to remove "obsolete knowledge" when they put together new entries. As though *what once was* can no longer be considered "science". Think about writing history with the same criterion.

251.   What kind of thinking would be comparable to the "mending of nets".

252.   The "little idyll" which carries (with a measure of relativity) the pattern and form of the qasida.

253.   *Rahil* (you noted) the entire span of the journey from here outward.   Because spill is essential.

254.   Stopping-points along the way, yes. But remember, the journey isn't that of a pilgrim.

255.   What is the smallest unit one can still measure. The basic items in the refurbishing of the world.   Via these dry bones.

256.   The line is built with nouns.   A concatenation of nouns.   A chain like a caravan of camels.   Like a constellation of marks within a tattoo.

257.   Beyond the dragnet of *qasida*, if something is projected, it's longing.   A multi-headed dragon, or the course of a rapid river.   Here, dam it up, it breaks out into seven streams.

258.   Desire is what the poet-hero-subject embodies. Always forward-urging, toward the nearby stopping places. But image and metaphor provide a redundance

of braided ties and conjunction. Lines of divergence, loops in the net, criss-cross each and every site.

259. The constant motion of desiring language, found in everything. Deviant, erring, idiosyncratic, packed with scandal. *Qasida*, one possible path, "exemplary" of the devious puzzle of desire.

260. Maybe even before the storm starts they'll give shelter. Or as it spreads. Or else we'd be left to the lashing rain.

261. The splitting of the subject-poet-hero, pursued by absence and lack (this is the poverty of the available), looking for the "not-I", read "other", in order to get from it a renewed promise of its own skin. Unconditional surrender is required. Say it this-just-once-more, "yes".

262. Acupuncture of the body because of thought's arrows. St. Sebastian riddled with imperatives of "Body, remember".

263.   Try it out, they say, on your skin, "and with the very scale I measure, measured".
What's nuttier. Lovers on the dunes wrapped around each other like a pair of ghost crabs from what hole presently surprised, or a rocking rhythm *naqa*-borne, a lurch of jolted fucking, a hump-backed supporting of the canopied fornicators.

264.   *Nasib.* Think of a line on a map erasing a sign to indicate that it's empty.

265.   Desire is form's being, oil for the bonfire. I mean the qasida.

GLOSSARY

atlal: the abodes, marks, and traces of the beloved's abandoned campsite.

baliyya: the ghost mare, the fallen hero's *naqa*, tethered to his tomb and abandoned.

fakhr: the boast, the third major movement of the qasida, often including wine song, *naqa* sacrifice, depiction of the poet-hero on horseback, battle-boast, and tribal boast.

karim: an untranslatable term usually rendered as "generous" or "noble": the centerpiece of tribal ethos, symbolized through the *naqa* sacrifice and the feeding of the tribe, the unflinching defense of the clan in battle, the lavish wine bouts and banquets, and, in a more abstract sense, the refusal to hoard one's life....

naqa: the camel mare, the poet-hero's mount during

the journey and sacrificial victim during the major pre-Islamic rite, the *naqa* sacrifice.

nasib: remembrance of the lost beloved, the first section of the qasida.

rahil: the journey, the second major movement of the qasida.

za'n: the departure of the beloved and the women in her tribe and the depiction of their howdahs, the richly decorated litters carried on camel stallions.

———————

(Definitions are taken from *Desert Tracings: Six Classic Arabian Odes,* translated and introduced by Michael Sells (Wesleyan University Press, 1989).